IMAGES · FROM · THE

I CHING

Visual Meditations on The Book of Change

IMAGES · FROM · THE
I CHING

Visual Meditations on The Book of Change

Paintings by Ann Williams
Introduction by Ralph Metzner

PRISM
PRESS

First published in Australia in 1987 by Craftsman House.
This edition published in Great Britain by
Prism Press, 2 South Street, Bridport,
Dorset DT6 3NQ, England,
and distributed in the United States of America by
the Avery Publishing Group Inc., 350 Thorens Avenue,
Garden City Park, New York 11040.

ISBN 1 85327 003 2

Editor	Nevill Drury
Design	Craig Peterson
Art	Craig Peterson and Catherine Martin
Typesetter	Deblaere Typesetting Pty. Limited, Sydney
Printer	Kyodo, Singapore

This book is dedicated to my twin Wendy, with thanks to my family, friends and teachers around the world

Ann Williams

CONTENTS

Introduction by Ralph Metzner

The *I Ching* is the oldest existing written formulation of the animistic, alchemical, organic philosophy known as Taoism, which stretches back 5000 years or more in an unbroken, though often submerged tradition, that is still very much alive to this day. This practical book of wisdom teachings has inspired thousands of volumes of commentaries – both in China, the land of its arising, and in other countries of the world. Although its purported use as a handbook of divination has undoubtedly contributed to its popularity and longevity, some scholars assert that the divinatory aspect of the book is merely a front, so to speak, or a package, for the esoteric philosophical teachings it is propounding.

Many contemporary admirers of the *I Ching* don't use it for divination, but read it like an inspirational religio-philosophical tract. Western mathematicians and philosophers, starting with Leibnitz in the 17th century, have occupied themselves with the mathematical structure and logic of the *I Ching*. There is a book on the correlation between the 64 hexagrams and the 64 triplet nucleic acid combinations that make up the genetic code on the double helix of the DNA molecule. And there have been numerous applications of the book to calendrical, astrological and numerological cycles.

To this day, in the West, new translations, versions, explanations and the like, appear at the rate of several distinct volumes or works, by different authors or translators, *each year*. The *I Ching* has inspired visual interpretations by painters and photographers – and to my mind, the paintings of Ann Williams presented in this volume are the finest and aesthetically most pleasing that I have seen.

It is widely thought that the Book of Changes *(I Ching)* and the Taoist philosophy it embodies are fundamentally concerned with the complementary interplay of two polar forces *yang* and *yin*. Though this is true, it is perhaps not generally appreciated that this duality presupposes a unitive principle that is the source and support of the opposites emerging from it. 'That which lets now the dark, now the light appear, is *Tao*.' *Tao* is the 'way', the matrix of change and possibility, that contains and gives birth to the light and dark energies. Without the experience of unity, the opposites conflict and diverge; by balancing them we attune to the inherent harmony. Thus we have a trinity: the two *(yin* and *yang)* balance and complement each other in the one *(tao)*.

The threefold unity of forces has been a central feature of Asian wisdom teachings and the perennial philosophy. In Indian mythology the threefold was personified in the trinity of supreme deities: Brahma the Creator, Shiva the Transformer, and Vishnu the Preserver. Christianity refers to the Holy Trinity as 'three in one' – the Father, the Son, and the Holy Spirit. G. I. Gurdjieff formulated a Law of Three: the interaction in all phenomena of the affirming force, the denying force, and the reconciling or equalising force. Though rarely recognised as such, modern physics also has a similar tri-une formula in Einstein's equation $E = mc^2$, which says in effect that energy can manifest inter-convertibly as matter (dark) or as radiation (light).

The experience of unity has not been common in the West until recently, when with the advent of psychedelics in the sixties, and of Asian meditation practices in the seventies, a perception of the under-lying oneness of all phenomena and life-forms has become accessible to many persons. In searching for an intellectual understanding of such experienced unity, not much help can be found in modern Western philosophy – one would have to go back to the medieval mystics such as Eckhart and the Neoplatonist philosophers such as Plotinus. It is my belief that the extraordinary and enduring popularity of the *I Ching* is due in part to the fact that it presents a way in which the experienced oneness, the *Tao*, through the dual forces and the threefold fusion, can be related to the manifold forms of life, to the 'ten thousand creatures', and to the ethical and social decisions we confront in everyday life.

How the *I Ching* does this is not at all easy to understand. It seems clear that it functions, among other things, as a convenient framework for intuition, much as do the Tarot, astrology, and other divinatory systems. After all, every 'reading' has to be interpreted by the questioner. Yet one wonders how the judgements and images were finally related to the particular patterns of lines obtained by throwing the coins or sorting the stalks. Were the 'holy sages' who composed the basic text clairvoyants who saw the actual patterned cycles of change and were able to code them in combinations of broken and solid lines? According to Chinese tradition, it was the legendary Fu Hsi, who lived perhaps in the 3rd or 4th millenium BC, who is pictured as having horns (thus indicating his nature and status as master shaman), and who taught the people the arts of hunting and fishing, who is said to have invented the system of using ▬ ▬ and ▬▬▬ to indicate *yin* and *yang* respectively. Some say he got the idea by observing the patterns of lines on a tortoise shell.

Originally, the terms *yang* and *yin* were used to designate the day-night cycle. Later, the concept was extended by subsequent genera-tions of Confucian and Taoist scholars, to include primal polarities on many levels: light-dark, firm-yielding, movement-rest, creative-recep-tive, male-female, odd-even numbers, involvement-detachment, essence-life, activity-stillness, unity-duality, primordial-conditioned, celestial-mundane, mind-body, reason-desire, effort-relaxation. 'In a state of rest the Creative is one, and in a state of motion it is straight...

the Receptive is closed in a state of rest, and in a state of motion it opens.' One could add 'positive-negative' to the above list of pairs of opposites – as long as it is remembered that this does not have an evaluative connotation, but rather carries the meaning of positive and negative electrical charge, coded + (plus) and − (minus).

Divinatory or mantic procedures such as the *I Ching*, the Tarot, astrology, and parapsychological phenomena which are inexplicable in terms of the causal determinative theories of modern science, are what induced C. G. Jung to formulate his principle of *synchronicity*, which he termed an 'acausal connecting principle'. The lawful connection between any two or more events, e.g. a life situation and an *I Ching* hexagram, is due, in this theory, not to a causal relationship between them, but by a non-random coincidence of meaning. By formulating this principle Jung is in effect saying that such divinations or 'psi hits' are not mere coincidences, but lawful, yet unpredictable synchronicities: they are simultaneous occurrences systematically related by inner meaning. The *Book of Changes* is seen by Jung as embodying this principle of synchronicity, which parallels the ancient and medieval Hermetic doctrine of correspondences. 'In the West', according to Jung, 'this thinking has been absent from the history of philosophy since the time of Heraclitus, and only reappears as a faint echo in Leibnitz.'

Heraclitus, who said 'you cannot step twice into the same river', and 'change alone is unchanging', formulated a philosophy based on the notion that everything is in flux, which is a simple version of the fundamental law of cyclic transformations that underlies the *I Ching*. Leibnitz in fact came into contact with the *I Ching* in one of the most interesting synchronistic events in the history of ideas: the mathematically logical ordering system of the 64 hexagrams invented or discovered by the 11th century Sung Dynasty scholar Shao Yung was brought to the attention of Leibnitz in the 17th century by Father Joachim Bouvet, a Jesuit missionary in China. Leibnitz found in Shao Yung's *I Ching* system an independent confirmation of his system of binary number notation, which uses combinations of 0 to 1 to express all numbers. He equated the *I Ching's* double *yin* line (━ ━) with 0, and the single *yang* line (━━━) with 1. In his philosophy Leibnitz identified 0 with the nothingness of unformed chaos, and 1 with God – and recommended that this equation be used by the missionaries for purposes of evangelisation. Since the binary number system underlies all digital computer programming, via on-off circuitry, the fundamental structure of the *I Ching* is congruent in this way with the computer technology of the 20th century.

According to the Taoist conceptions, *yang* force goes out to a maximum, like the crest of a wave, and then turns, softens, yields, declines into *yin*, just as the noontime sun, after reaching its zenith, begins to sink back down into darkness, and like the midsummer *yang* sun that begins to turn southward with longer *yin* nights, right after peaking at the solstice. The *yin* force, at its extreme, coalesces and becomes firmly *yang*, just as the sun at midnight, after reaching its nadir, begins to re-ascend toward the morning light, and like the sun at the midwinter solstice passing through the longest dark *yin* night, turns northward again with longer *yang* days.

An *I Ching* commentary says: 'There is therefore in the Changes the Great Primal Beginning *(t'ai chi)*. This generates the two primary forces. The two primary forces generate the four images (the moving and resting *yin* and *yang* lines). The four images generate the eight trigrams.' *Tai ch'i* is literally 'the great ridgepole'. This term also appears in the alchemical yogic text, *The Secret of the Golden Flower*, where it refers to the central vertical axis of the human body, which is the pivot of inner alchemical work. At the macrocosmic level the great ridgepole is most likely the vertical axis of the earth, whose rotation on that axis generates the light and dark phases of the diurnal cycle.

The sixty-four hexagram signs that constitute the *I Ching* are made up of all possible combinations of trigram (three-line) signs. These eight trigrams are the basic symbolic alphabet of the *Book of Changes* – their many levels of meaning, when combined in pairs, yield an almost limitless variety of possible interpretations. The eight trigrams are based on the fact that eight is the number of combinations of two types of lines (━ ━ and ━━) in triads. Why triads? The two principles, *yin* and *yang*, are combined in triads to symbolise the mediating role of man (middle line) between heaven (top line) and earth (bottom line). In the hexagrams, the same principle of interpretation applies: the top two lines relate to heaven *(yang)*, the middle two to humanity, and the bottom two to earth *(yin)*.

The commentaries say: 'The Book of Changes contains the measure of heaven and earth; therefore it enables us to comprehend the *tao* of heaven and earth and its order. Looking upward, we contemplate with its help the signs in the heavens; looking downward we examine the lines of the earth... since in this way man comes to resemble heaven and earth, he is not in conflict with them. His wisdom embraces all things, and his *tao* brings order into the whole world.'

It is necessary to understand that the terms *heaven* and *earth* have esoteric as well as exoteric significance. On one level, the statement above says that by contemplating cosmic laws ('signs in the heavens') and the principles of mineral and biological order ('the lines of the earth'), we come to recognise how we as human beings are part of this unified, yet ever-changing pattern of relationships. This is the *I Ching's* formulation of the ancient principle of correspondence – the idea that man is a microcosm, exemplifying within himself the order of the macrocosm. On a deeper level, *heaven* is the world of spirit, or essence, and *earth* the world of matter, or life. So the statement tells us that by becoming aware of our spiritual essence and observing our physical nature we can bring ourselves into alignment: we 'come to resemble heaven and earth'. Thus we are attuned to the *tao*, and are freed from conflict and error.

The eight trigrams, and the hexagrams based on them, have many levels of meaning. These include aspects of Nature (e.g. earth, thunder, lake); general qualities or attributes (e.g. creative, gentle, abysmal); seasons of the year; times of the day; members of the family; parts of the body; and specific animals. Any given divinatory reading of the *I Ching* will be an intuitive selection and synthesis of any or all of these meanings. The paintings of Ann Williams likewise are the intuitively derived visual images inspired by the combinations of trigram symbols and the hexagram titles as given in modern English translations. Her primary focus seems to have been the Nature images, and how these combine in each hexagram. The result is an absorbing series of interior, visionary landscapes, pregnant with symbolic meanings.

One very interesting method for beginning to appreciate the meanings of the hexagrams is to look at those eight hexagrams that are the doubles of the eight basic trigrams, i.e. where both the upper and lower trigrams are the same. They are the following hexagrams: 1, 2, 51, 29, 52, 57, 30, and 58. The reader of this book might also find it meaningful to begin by looking at the images of these hexagrams, in which the basic trigrams are manifested at double strength, as it were, both 'above' and 'below'. In the following, we will review the symbolic associations of the eight basic elemental signs (trigrams), and examine the painter's visual rendering of the phase of change (hexagram) to which it corresponds. (I have added the corresponding signs of the Zodiac, as inferred from the seasonal King Wen arrangement of the trigrams, because there are remarkable symbolic connections, even although the Western Zodiac signs are quite different from the Chinese astrological system.)

is **Ch'ien**, three *yang* lines, the creative, heaven above, the father, the head, the horse. This has qualities of strength, firmness, dynamic energy, the cosmic masculine power; manifested in the daytime, and in the early winter season of later Scorpio and Sagittarius (a fire sign with associations of power and movement).

Ann's painting of hexagram #1 presents the shimmering cosmic dragon (which is the primary symbol of that hexagram). The dragon in Chinese tradition does not have associations of danger and destructiveness, as it does in the West; rather it is associated with lightning, and thought of as the fecundating creative power of cosmic and atmospheric energy streaming down to earth. The painting portrays a magnificent rainbow-hued, spiral-coiled dragon, an image of tremendous power.

━━ ━━ is **K'un**, three *yin* lines, the receptive, earth, the mother, the
━━ ━━ abdomen, the cow. The magnetic, yielding power of the female, with attributes of adaptability and nurturance; it is manifested in nighttime, and in the early autumn harvest season of later Leo and Virgo (an earth sign, the grain mother goddess).

The painting of hexagram #2 shows a russet brown desert landscape seen from above, with a ring-shaped mound like a crater. Inside the crater is a square frame with a picture of a desert landscape with a crater-ring, reproducing the larger picture, and inside the crater is another, even smaller square picture of a desert with a crater ring. In traditional Chinese symbolism the circle is earth and the square heaven. Thus, the two combined make a mandala of heaven-on-earth. Earth, which is body on the individual level, receives the seed of heaven, which is spirit on the individual level, and incorporates it into herself.

━━ ━━ is **Chen**, the arousing, thunder, the eldest son, the feet, the
━━━━ dragon. This is the fiery power of excitation, initiative, growth and expansion, manifested in the early morning, and in the late spring season of Aries (a fire sign) and early Taurus.

The painting of hexagram #51, which is double thunder, shows a stone wall with a dragon in bas-relief, with a great crack running down the wall; above the wall are thunder clouds. The image suggests sudden shock, break-up of structures, and a kind of violent kinetic energy. The dragon has a look of wide-eyed startle, like that of a man in a moment of shock of self recognition.

━━━━ is **Sun**, the gentle, wind and wood, the eldest daughter, the
━━ ━━ thighs, the cock. It has qualities of gently, persistently penetrating, like wind through the trees, flexibility and honesty. It manifests in the late morning, and in the early summer of late Taurus and Gemini (an air sign).

The painting of hexagram #57, which is double wind, shows a wood carving of a meditative buddha head, with an opening down the centre, as though an outer mask had been pulled back, to reveal another face within. The expression on both the outer and inner face is serene and gentle. The hand is held up in the teaching *mudra*, suggestive of the 'gentle influence' attribute of this hexagram.

☵ is **K'an**, the 'abysmal', deep canyon, water, the moon, the second son, the ears, the boar. It has qualities of danger, mystery, profundity, fearfulness. It manifests at around midnight in the diurnal cycle, and in later winter of Capricorn and early Aquarius (the water-bearer).

The hexagram for this sign doubled is #29, which in various translations has connotations of double water, danger, pitfall, abyss. Ann Williams' painting shows storm clouds above, with a cyclone waterspout arcing down into an ominous looking maelstrom in the ocean below. The feeling evoked is of being 'caught between the devil and the deep blue sea'.

☲ is **Li**, called 'the clinging', fire, the sun, the second daughter, the eyes, the bird. It has attributes of clarity, illumination, intelligence, consciousness and is associated with high noon in the diurnal cycle. In the seasonal cycle Li corresponds to the later summer of Cancer and the first part of Leo (a fire sign).

Hexagram #30, which is Li doubled, is interpreted as fire within and fire without, inner and outer illumination, enlightenment spreading to the four corners of the earth. The painter here gives us a bronze image of the Hindu sun deity, surmounting a chariot with twelve horses, each bearing a flame in a vessel, and surrounded by a halo of flame-coloured petals. One feels a driving momentum of tremendous brilliance, fanning out to the twelve sectors of the universe, unobstructed in its radiance.

☶ is **Ken**, the mountain, meditative stillness, the youngest son, the hands, the dog. It has qualities of tranquillity, immobility, calmness, resting, and is manifested around sunrise in the day cycle, and in the early spring season of later Aquarius and Pisces.

The corresponding hexagram and painting is #52, which shows a gigantic sculpture of a human figure set within an arch inside a mountain. This hexagram connotes the inner and outer stillness of meditation, where we maintain mountain-like stillness without, and stillness of the mind within. Only through such deep inner and outer tranquillity, can we attain to a realisation of our true nature.

☱ is **Tui**, the joyous, the lake, the youngest daughter, the mouth, the sheep. It has attributes of fullness, satisfaction, delight, openness, balance and pleasure, and is associated with the mellow time of sunset. In the seasonal cycle Tui corresponds to late autumn, the time of Libra (a Venus air sign of balance) and early Scorpio (also associated with sexuality).

The corresponding hexagram is #58, the double joyous lake, which in Ann Williams' paintings is a surreal image of an autumnal landscape with two small lakes, seen as from the air, each having the outline shape of a human figure. The two humanoid lakes are stretching out their arms to one another, as if to embrace, with one holding what might be a flower bunch. The feeling is one of joyousness, playfulness and delight.

The eight paintings described above, based on the doubling of the basic eight trigrams, out of a total of 64 possible combinations, are a gifted painter's sensitive interpretations of these ancient symbolic images. The creation and existence of such images must be considered part of the contemplative tradition of *I Ching* lore, rather than another formulation for divinatory purposes. I will conclude by quoting from the *Book of Balance and Harmony*, a famous compendium of Taoist teachings from the 13th-14th century Yuan Dynasty, which gives general guidelines for understanding the interaction of *yin* and *yang* energies in everyday life, and touches on many of the themes raised in this discussion:

'The waning and waxing of energy and matter are the movement and rest of things; rising and retiring by day and night are the movement and rest of the body. Everything, including the advance and retreat of the person, the arising and vanishing thoughts, the fortune and adversity of the world, the success and failure of tasks, is a matter of the alternating rise and fall of movement and rest.

If you observe their patterns of movement and rest, you can see the myriad changes of myriad events and the conditions of myriad beings. When you are mindful in times of rest, you are observant in times of movement. If you have self-mastery in times of rest, you can be decisive in times of movement. If you have stability in times of rest, actions will not lead to unfortunate results. Rest is the foundation of movement, movement is the potential of rest. When you do not lose the constant in movement and rest, your path will be illumined.'*

* From *The Taoist I Ching*, translated by Thomas Cleary (Boston: Shambhala, 1986), p. 9.

A Note on Practical Divination
by Ann Williams

For purposes of divination you will need to consult one of the many translations now available. My preference is for R. L. Wing's, *The I Ching Workbook* (Doubleday), Richard Wilhelm's *I Ching* or *Book of Changes* (Routledge & Kegan Paul) and John Blofeld's *I Ching, The Book of Change* (Unwin) – these are invaluable. Such books are necessary for an appreciation of the exact and specific direction to look for understanding and also generally include a more involved method of forecasting using yarrow stalks.

Ralph Metzner's introduction, happily included in this book, gives an admirably clear and succinct view of the underlying principles of the I Ching.

The Method

To discover the hexagram which describes your current sense of the world you will need three coins. Focus your attention, formulate your question carefully (do not expect a yes/no answer), and throw the three coins three times. This will give you the lower trigram. Another three throws gives the upper trigram. The sixty-four hexagrams upon which the forecasts are based are each composed of two trigrams making a total of six lines. Each throw produces a line building the hexagram from the bottom upwards. The transformation of one or more 'moving' lines into its opposite gives a second hexagram which modifies the meaning of the first. For example: Assign the value of 'heads' as *yin* 'tails' as *yang*:

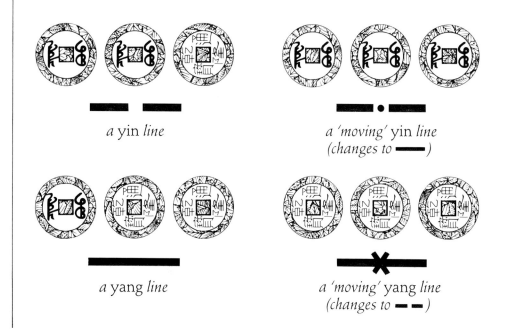

a yin *line*

a 'moving' yin *line*
(changes to ▬▬ *)*

a yang line

a 'moving' yang line
(changes to ▬ ▬ *)*

For example:

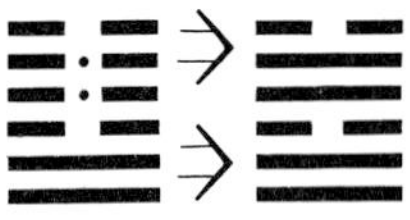

The first fall of the three coins represents the bottom line of the hexagram. Using the key find the lower trigram ☰ in the left column, then the upper trigram ☱ in the top column – where they intersect yields the number of the hexagram: 19, *Approach*.

19 changing to 58

Since there are 'moving' lines in the 4th and 5th place the resulting (2nd) hexagram is *58, The Joyous*. Refer to the appropriate text and commentaries in your preferred translation.

Practice, and a free use of the intuitive faculty when interpreting the response, will, for sure, give you fresh insights to your questions and an indication of why the *I Ching*, has been in living use for millennia.

Key to locating the hexagram

TRIGRAMS

Upper

Lower								
	1	34	5	26	11	9	14	43
	25	51	3	27	24	42	21	17
	6	40	29	4	7	59	64	47
	33	62	39	52	15	53	56	31
	12	16	8	23	2	20	35	45
	44	32	48	18	46	57	50	28
	13	55	63	22	36	37	30	49
	10	54	60	41	19	61	38	58

THE IMAGES AND HEXAGRAMS

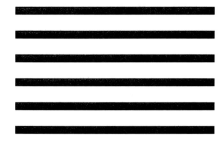

1. The Creative
Heaven over Heaven

Access one moment from the
scintillating play of consciousness
– The Creative.
Dragon power shimmers in
the Heavens; anything you wish
may happen

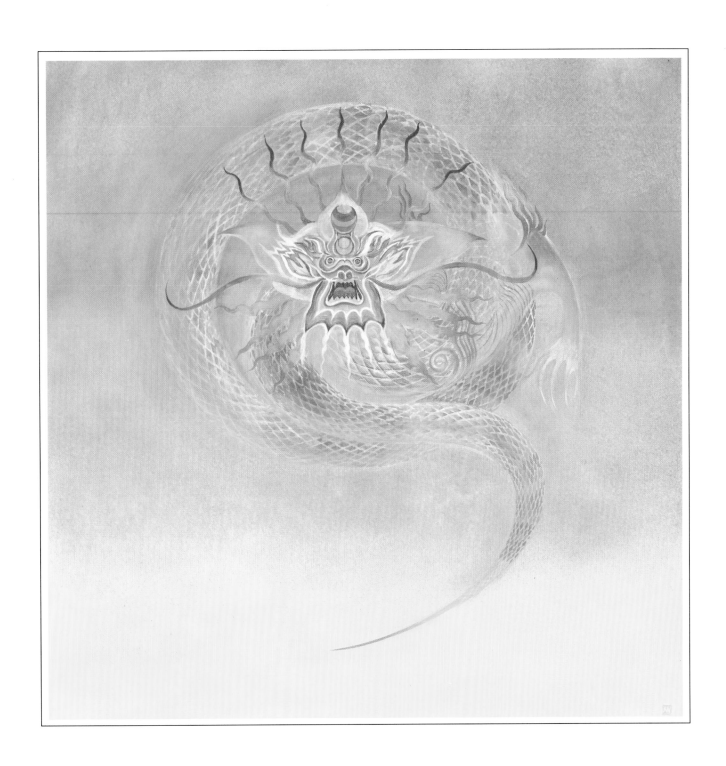

Heaven over Heaven

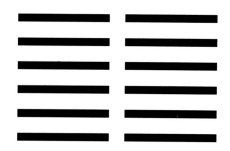

2. The Receptive
Earth over Earth

Sensing the Earth, Centre; be receptive
to Gaia's gifts

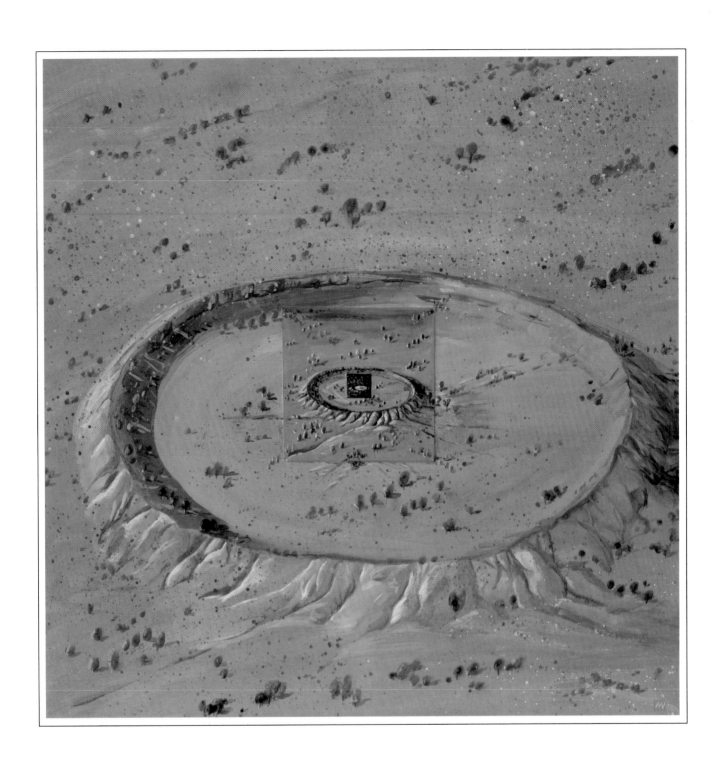

Earth over Earth

3. Difficult Beginnings
Water over Thunder

Whole landscapes emerge from
the depths. New life struggles into
being; difficult beginnings

Water over Thunder

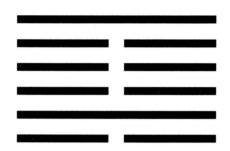

4. Inexperience
Mountain over Water

Mountainous waves crest,
unconscious surges inform.
Inexperience must seek a teacher

Mountain over Water

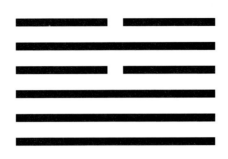

5. Calculated Inaction
Water over Heaven

Halt and wait, dispelling fear. Know
this for a time of calculated inaction

Water over Heaven

6. Conflict
Heaven over Water

In your own brain feel the
dichotomy of that which sees and that
which names. Resolve the inner conflict

Heaven over Water

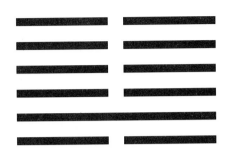

7. Collective Force
Earth over Water

The battle between the forces
of light and darkness is part of Vishnu's
great dream. Collective force seeks
a worthy leader

Earth over Water

8. Unity
Water over Earth

Nature's calligraphy sings a soft
song of unity

Water over Earth

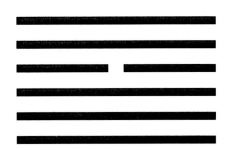

9. Restrained
Wind over Heaven

Gently open the windows of your mind

Wind over Heaven

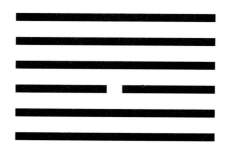

10. Conduct
Heaven over Lake

Simply, cheerfully treading a
level course between Heaven's hem
and tiger's tail

Heaven over Lake

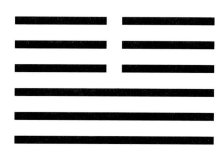

11. Peace
Earth over Heaven

Heaven and Earth join hands;
peacefulness pervades

Earth over Heaven

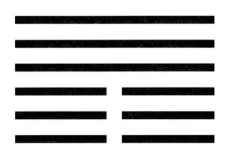

12. Stagnation
Heaven over Earth

The creative and the receptive
pull apart – wherever this occurs,
a period of stagnation

Heaven over Earth

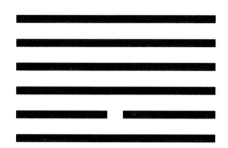

13. Community
Heaven over Fire

See the flowers bloom in the
warmth of heartfelt community

Heaven over Fire

14. Sovereignty
Fire over Heaven

Clarity with creative power;
Shiva dances and we all can feel the
fierce glitter of sovereignty

Fire over Heaven

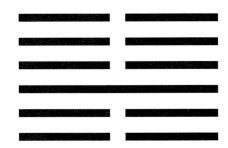

15. **Moderation**
Earth over Mountain

Simply standing in the middle,
modestly

Earth over Mountain

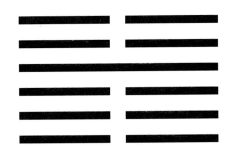

16. Enthusiasm
Thunder over Earth

Celestial apsaras harmonise.
Even now, listen with enthusiasm

Thunder over Earth

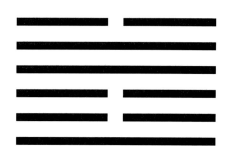

17. Adapting
Lake over Thunder

Underwater tendrils interwine a sign
of adamantine clarity. Adapt to the flow

Lake over Thunder

18. Repair
Mountain over Wind

Perishable palettes, our part in
these cycles of decay and repair

Mountain over Wind

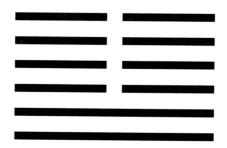

19. Approach
Earth over Lake

A stone staircase awaits the
approach of joy. The balance between
steps – ascending

Earth over Lake

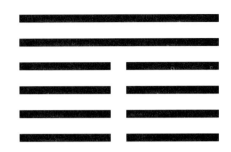

20. Contemplating
Wind over Earth

Contemplating timelessly, observing
and transforming. He sways the people

Wind over Earth

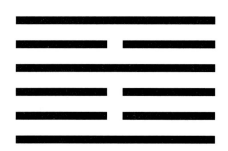

21. Reform
Fire over Thunder

King of demons, Rawana burns
away dark deeds and thoughts.
Reform is vital

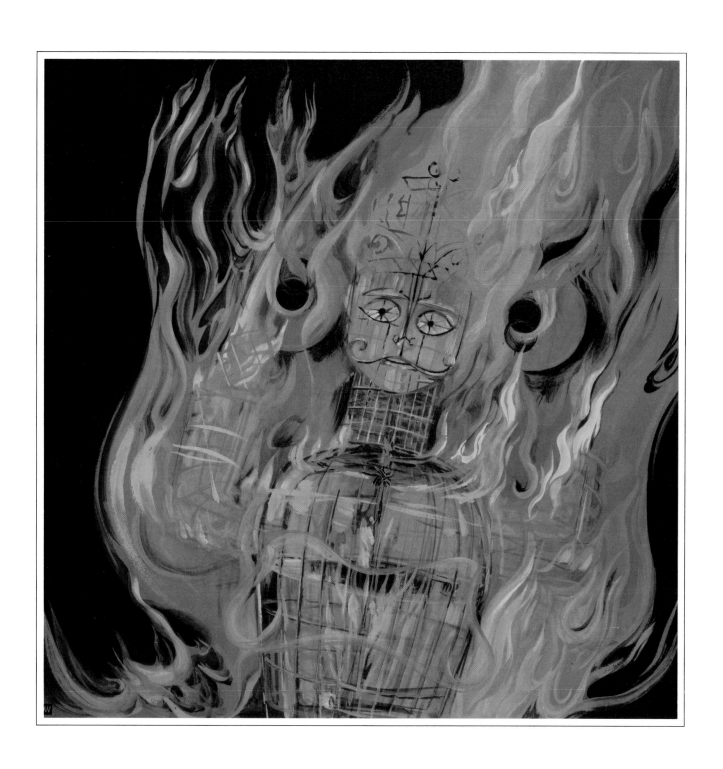

Fire over Thunder

22. Grace
Mountain over Fire

Within us, a fire of brightness.
Keeping still, watching the sunset
– gracefully

Mountain over Fire

23. Deterioration
Mountain over Earth

Heed Earth's depleted sighs
– they are your own

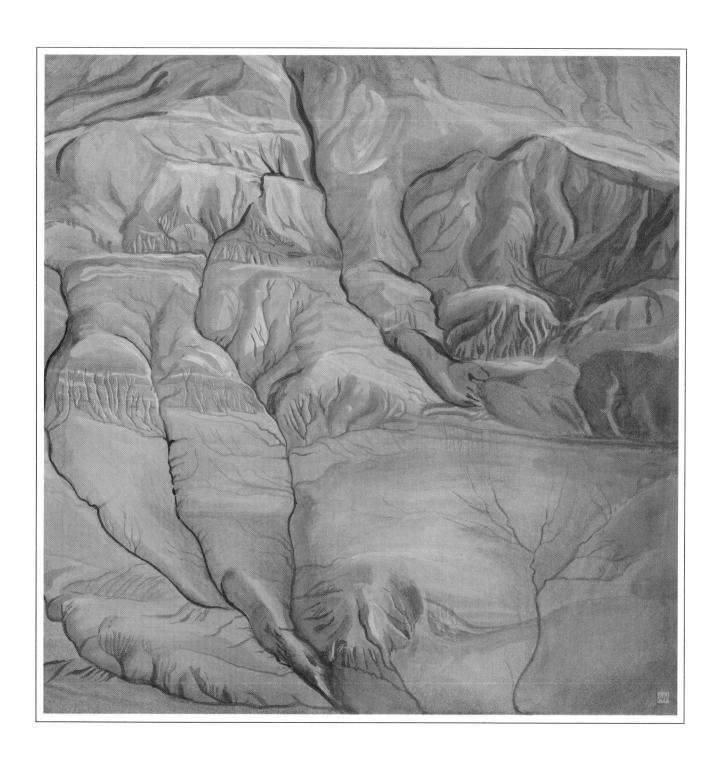

Mountain over Earth

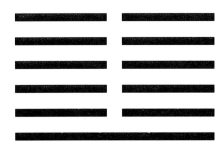

24. Return
Earth over Thunder

Listen to the mind's footsteps
returning. Why is this learning cycle
repeating?

Earth over Thunder

25. Innocence
Heaven over Thunder

Innocently hovering above
thunder heads; sense spontaneous
action arising

Heaven over Thunder

26. Potential Energy
Mountain over Heaven

Heaven reflects in the landscape;
mountains are carved in time.
Steps of energy, past and future

Mountain over Heaven

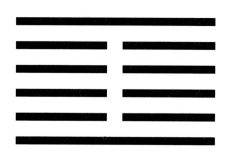

27. Nourishing
Mountain over Thunder

In quest of the necessities of mind
and body, I come across a rainbow

Mountain over Thunder

28. Excess
Lake over Wind

Bright parrots of joy – even one in
the hand could be an excess. Between,
enough, and too much – how far?

Lake over Wind

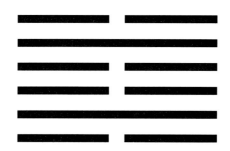

29. The Abyss
Water over Water

A surreal sea for this dangerous
journey upwards

Water over Water

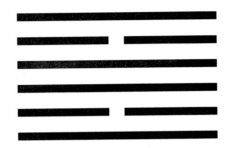

30. The Clinging
Fire over Fire

Surya the Sun God urges the
brightness onwards

Fire over Fire

31. Attraction
Lake over Mountain

From the big toe energy rises
like a snake, attracting her mate

Lake over Mountain

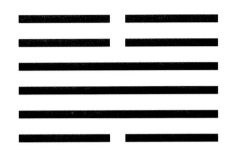

32. Enduring
Thunder over Wind

Remote sentinels. On the
plains of endurance, they continue

Thunder over Wind

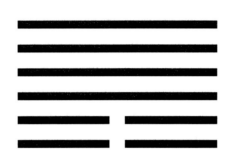

33. Retreat
Heaven over Mountain

Even in retreat, on the edge
of mirage a god's name is hidden

Heaven over Mountain

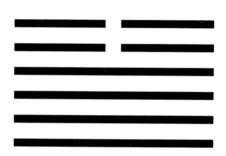

34. Great Power
Thunder over Heaven

Portents of great power rising
in the sky one afternoon

Thunder over Heaven

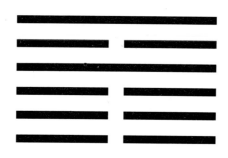

35. Progress
Fire over Earth

Touch the earth, feel a clear fire
rising and opening into light

Fire over Earth

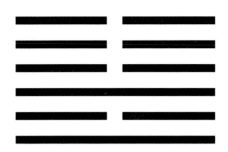

36. Censorship
Earth over Fire

Imprisoned in self-censoring,
how do we break free?

Earth over Fire

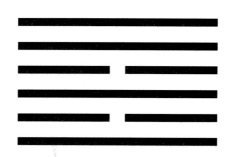

37. Family
Wind over Fire

Father, mother, brother, sister,
male, female. In each, these polarities

Wind over Fire

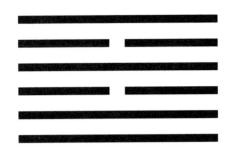

38. Opposition
Fire over Lake

Balancing the eternal opposites –
before a tiger bars the way

Fire over Lake

39. Obstacles
Water over Mountain

A thousand miles of obstacles
in these inner seas

Water over Mountain

40. Liberation
Thunder over Water

One hand claps, the Buddha turns
the wheel, each green moment frees

Thunder over Water

41. Decrease
Mountain over Lake

Reducing one's needs at the declining
edge; realising simplicity

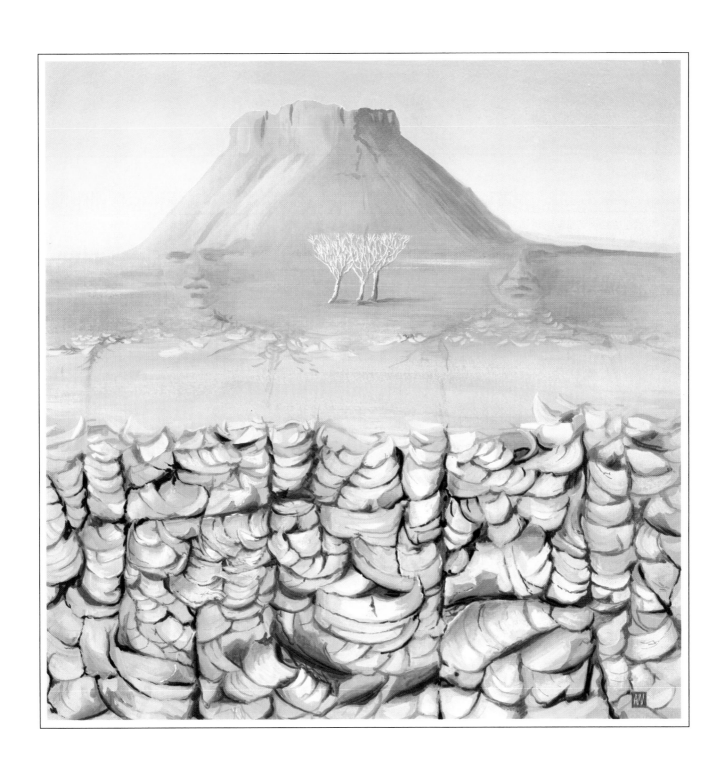

Mountain over Lake

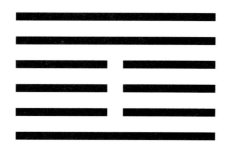

42. Increase
Wind over Thunder

Spreading my arms,
embracing generosity

Wind over Thunder

43. Breakthrough
Lake over Heaven

Fish swim in the sky
and my wings break through all barriers

Lake over Heaven

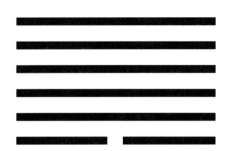

44. **Temptation**
Heaven over Wind

Amazed, I meet myself
coming from the centre

Heaven over Wind

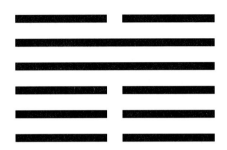

45. Assembling
Lake over Earth

The group assembles. We watch the
foam-flecked tracks with pleasure

Lake over Earth

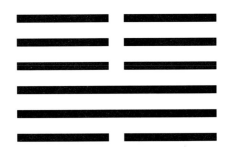

46. Ascending
Earth over Wind

Ascending like the excitement
of Spring, colouring the earth

Earth over Wind

47. Adversity
Lake over Water

Riding out the tide of adversity;
remaining mindful

Lake over Water

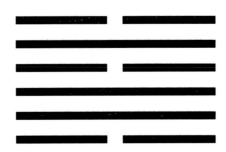

48. The Source
Water over Wind

Attuned to the Source; the delight
of quenching thirst inexhaustibly

Water over Wind

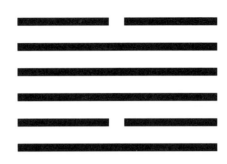

49. Changing
Lake over Fire

Water snakes slide upright before
a flaming bow; this also will change

Lake over Fire

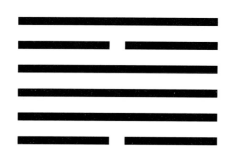

50. Cosmic Order
Fire over Wind

Lighting incense at an altar to the
Numinous, I see the flower

Fire over Wind

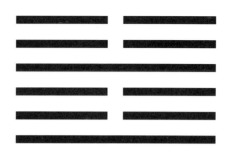

51. Shocking
Thunder over Thunder

The breath of the dragon comes
fast and shocking; his heart must open

Thunder over Thunder

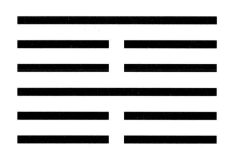

52. Keeping Still
Mountain over Mountain

Keeping still, forever! To fully sense,
'I am that' — should it take so long?

Mountain over Mountain

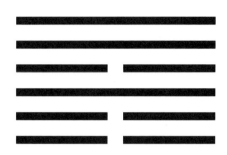

53. **Development**
Wind over Mountain

Floating gradually by one
of my windows, watching the
mountains grow

Wind over Mountain

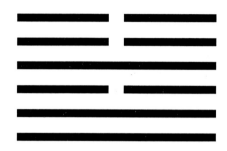

54. Subordinate
Thunder over Lake

Bending low, lower, below the volcano

Thunder over Lake

55. Zenith
Thunder over Fire

To be fully aware at the summit
of power – the essence of achievement

Thunder over Fire

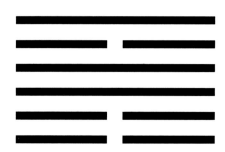

56. Traveller
Fire over Mountain

Fire over mountain – a bird's nest
burns and even the cacti are messengers
along the upward path

Fire over Mountain

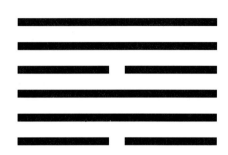

57. Penetrating Influence
Wind over Wind

Looking inward, I become the
picture of an old timber carving,
looking inward

Wind over Wind

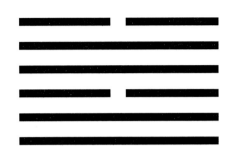

58. The Joyous
Lake over Lake

Bearing a gift of flowers, I leap
across a clear lake of joy

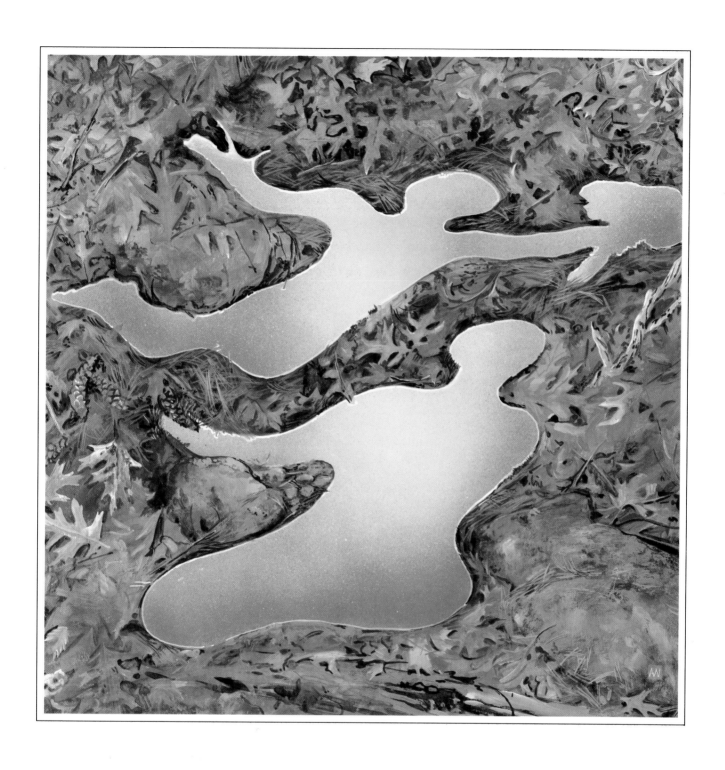

Lake over Lake

59. Dispersion
Wind over Water

Dispersing thoughts like birds;
seeking the return to wholeness

Wind over Water

60. **Limitation**
Water over Lake

Limited in time and space,
a dragon flickers at lake's edge.
See how we restrict ourselves!

Water over Lake

61. Insight
Wind over Lake

Let my mind follow attentively,
each moment, as from a seed to a full
flowering – insight

Wind over Lake

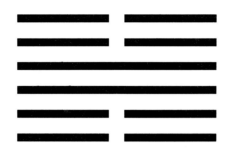

62. Conscientiousness
Thunder over Mountain

Unexpected insights from being
small and still

Thunder over Mountain

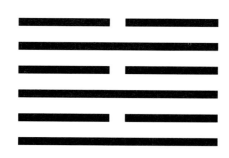

63. After Completion
Water over Fire

Intimations of a fiery heart between
frozen faced whispers of leavetaking;
completion edges into transition

Water over Fire

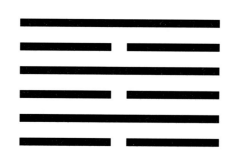

64. Before Completion
Fire over Water

From the seed of an idea,
a multitude. Seeing where we've been,
where headed, the Sun rises from
the sea – reborn

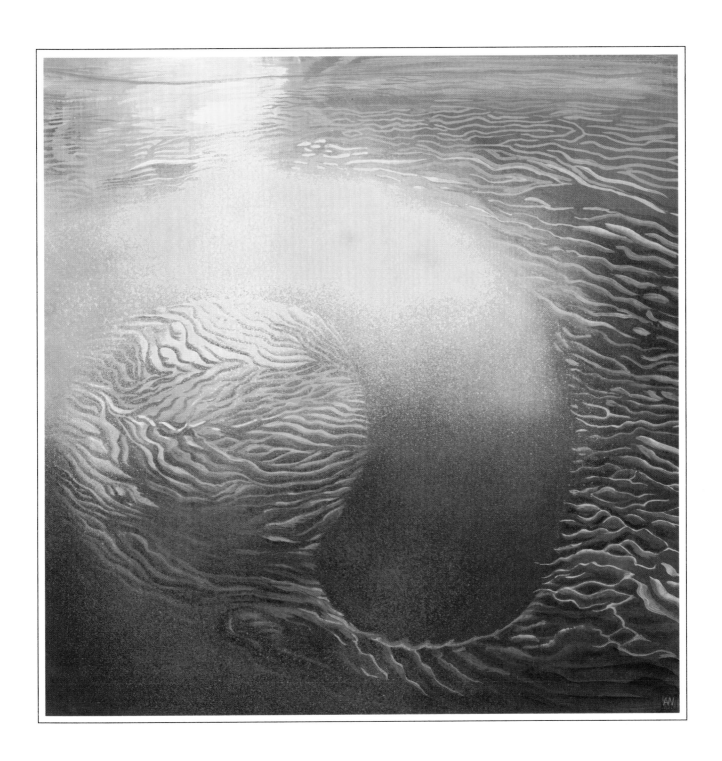

Fire over Water

The Artist and Author

Ann Williams was born in 1942 and grew up in the Australian outback. She worked as a graphic designer for twelve years and had her first exhibition of paintings in 1970.

She has lived in the Indian Himalayas for five years and has travelled extensively in Asia, Europe and North America. These journeys, and an active interest in Vipassana meditation and Transpersonal psychology are her main creative inspiration.

Ralph Metzner, PhD, has been an internationally recognised researcher and teacher in the area of consciousness for over 25 years. He is the author of such books as *Maps of Consciousness, Know Your Type* and *Opening to Inner Light* and is Professor of East-West Psychology at the California Institute of Integral Studies in San Francisco.